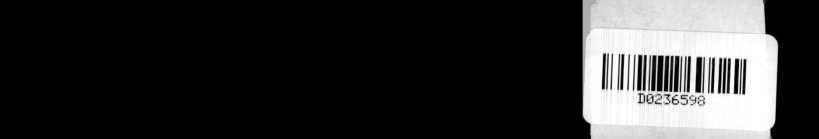

SOUND TRACKERS – ROCK 'N' ROLL
was produced by

David West Children's Books
5-11 Mortimer Street
London W1N 7RH

Picture research: Brooks Krikler Research

First published in Great Britain in 1998 by
Heinemann Library, Halley Court, Jordan Hill, Oxford OX2 8EJ, a division of
Reed Educational and Professional Publishing Limited.

OXFORD MELBOURNE AUCKLAND KUALA LUMPUR
SINGAPORE IBADAN NAIROBI KAMPALA JOHANNESBURG
GABORONE PORTSMOUTH NH CHICAGO

Copyright © 1998 David West Children's Books

01 00 99 98
10 9 8 7 6 5 4 3 2 1

ISBN 0 431 09102 1 (HB)
ISBN 0 431 09106 4 (PB)

British Library Cataloguing in Publicaton Data

Brunning, Bob
Rock 'n' roll. – (Sound trackers)
1. Rock music – Juvenile literature
I. Title
781. 6 ' 6

Printed and bound in Italy.

Rock 'n' Roll

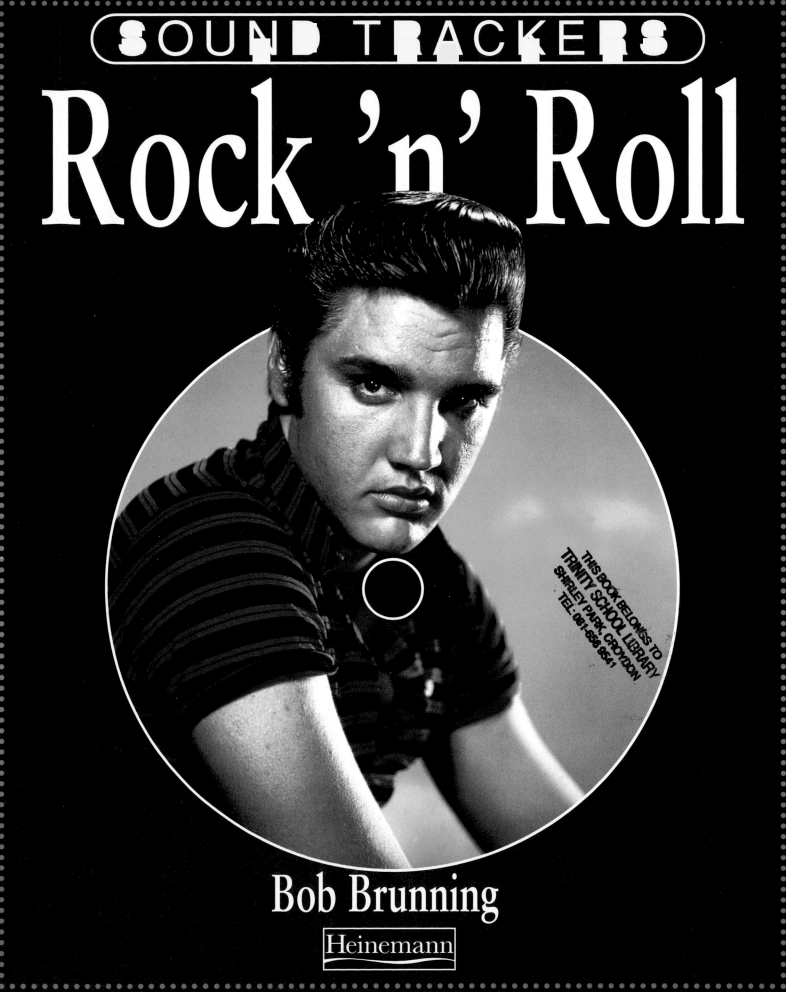

Bob Brunning

Heinemann

CONTENTS

On these discs is a selection of the artists' recordings. Many of these albums are now available on CD. If they are not, many of the tracks from them can be found on compilation CDs.

Chuck Berry

These boxes give you extra information about the artists and their times.

Some contain anecdotes about the artists themselves or about the people who helped their careers or, occasionally, about those who exploited them.

Others provide historical facts about the music, lifestyles, fans and fashions of the day.

INTRODUCTION

In the mid-1950s a New York disc jockey, Alan Freed, invented the term 'rock 'n' roll' for a new, exciting music he was beginning to play on his popular radio station.

Loud, brash, with a very strong beat, rock and roll was aimed at a new group of people: teenagers. Before the 1950s young people did not have their own music, clothes and fads but were just younger versions of their parents. That was about to change.

Bill Haley's 'Rock Around The Clock' is arguably the best-known anthem of rock 'n' roll music. It has sold over 20 million copies.

Alan Freed and many other disc jockeys in the USA started to play music that the grown-ups did not approve of. Black singers like Chuck Berry, Fats Domino, Little Richard, Bo Diddley and many others were producing music based on their powerful rhythm and blues gospel roots. White performers were mixing all those influences with country and western and soul music.

Elvis Presley, Buddy Holly, Gene Vincent, Eddie Cochran and dozens of other performers started to make records for young people. They sang about teenagers' problems – with parents, boyfriends/girlfriends, school, money. In the UK artists like Cliff Richard, Marty Wilde, Billy Fury and Tommy Steele did the same.

Rock and roll music is as popular today as when it burst into people's lives over 40 years ago. Parents then dismissed it as a five minute wonder. A long five minutes!

CHUCK BERRY

What sets Chuck Berry apart from most of the rock 'n' roll stars of the 1950s and '60s was that he was a very accomplished songwriter. Performers like Elvis Presley, Little Richard, Buddy Holly and many others relied upon professional songwriters to provide them with the material to record. Berry wrote his own songs, dealing entertainingly with the problems of relationships, parents, school, cars, cash flow – all the things that teenagers in the USA were worrying about.

GETTING STARTED

Born in 1926 in San Jose, California, Charles Edward Berry moved to St. Louis, Missouri, as a child and sang in his church and school choir in his teens. He trained as a hairdresser and played for fun with a trio at weekends. In 1955, when he was nearly 30 years old, he recorded a couple of his own songs and moved to Chicago, the centre for blues music at the time. He searched out blues legend Muddy Waters, who introduced him to Leonard Chess, owner of the Chess record label. Chess listened to Chuck's two songs and released both of them.

'One Dozen Berrys'
November '58
'After School Sessions'
June '58

'The Collection'
June '88
'Chuck Berry Boxed Set'
November '89

'Maybellene', a witty song about a boy who chases his two-timing girlfriend, went straight to the top of the rhythm and blues (R&B) charts.

THE GUITAR GOES ELECTRIC

The electric guitar was developed in the USA during the 1930s and '40s. With the need to project a louder but tonally accurate sound, early versions appeared as electric–acoustic guitars, like the Rickenbacker Electro Spanish model, made in the early '30s. They were conventional acoustic guitars with electric pickups and associated controls built in.

In 1931 a prototype instrument was built by George Beauchamp, Paul Barth and Harry Watson which consisted of a solid, round body with pickup attached. It looked like a banjo and was nicknamed 'The Frying Pan'.

The solid body proved better, preventing unwanted interference from the 'hollow' body of the acoustic and so in 1950 Fender introduced the world's first commercially available solid body electric guitar (right), called the Fender Broadcaster.

This paved the way for rock musicians the world over.

Chuck Berry's career was launched, his music a mixing of blues, country and western (C&W), R&B and rock and roll.

Berry in the film, 'Hail, Hail, Rock 'n' Roll'.

SUCCESS

Berry put his finger firmly on the pulse of the worries of a generation. He recorded dozens of his own songs, many of them complete short stories. He was an innovative guitarist and also developed his famous duckwalk – while playing, he would walk across the stage in a peculiar, bent-kneed style. He charged promoters extra to perform this manoeuvre!

The singles 'Brown Eyed Handsome Man', 'Roll Over Beethoven' (later recorded by the Beatles), 'Sweet Little Sixteen', 'Too Much Monkey Business', 'Johnny B. Good', 'School Days' and 'No Money Down' made Chuck Berry a popular and wealthy entertainer by the '60s.

BAD TIMES

Too soon it started to go wrong. Chuck was imprisoned between 1962 and '64 and despite quickly releasing three more classic singles, 'Nadine', 'No Particular Place To Go' and 'You Can Never Tell', he never regained his earlier level of international success. Berry continued to tour the world, although he sometimes lacked his previous dynamism. In 1972 he achieved his first No. 1 single on both sides of the Atlantic with 'Ding A Ling', although the song was certainly not one of his best.

In 1987, Chuck Berry featured in the film documentary 'Hail, Hail, Rock 'n' Roll', in which an exasperated Keith Richards (guitarist in the Rolling Stones) tries to persuade a stubborn Berry to improve his rather sloppy stage performance.

Berry plays with Richards in 'Hail, Hail, Rock 'n' Roll'.

STILL GOING STRONG

In 1998, at the age of 72, Chuck Berry continues to tour the world, performing some of the very best rock 'n' roll songs ever written – one of the true rock 'n' roll greats.

EDDIE COCHRAN

On 16 April 1960 Eddie Cochran took a taxi from Bristol in order to catch his plane home after his successful UK tour. With him were Gene Vincent and Cochran's girlfriend, Sharon Sheely. A tyre blew, the car crashed into a lamp post, and 16 hours later Eddie Cochran died from severe head injuries. Ironically, he had escaped death just one year earlier, when he had turned down the chance of appearing in the 'US Winter Dance Party Tour', featuring Buddy Holly, Ritchie Valens and The Big Bopper. All three died when their light plane crashed shortly after take-off from Iowa on 3 February 1959.

KEEN TEEN

Edward Ray Cochran was born in Oklahoma in 1938. As a teenager he became very interested in music and after flirting with several instruments decided the guitar was what he wanted to play. In 1955 he formed the 'Cochrans' with friend Hank Cochran (no relation). A year later Jerry Capeheart joined the duo. They made various records, none of which were commercially successful. Hank left the trio. Eddie and Jerry's first co-written song, 'Skinny Jim', was not a hit – but Eddie Cochran was just about to get his extremely lucky break.

Cochran, with obligatory slicked-back hair, belts out some rock 'n' roll with gusto.

THE BREAK

Cochan was asked to sing 'Twenty Flight Rock' in the film, 'The Girl Can't Help It'. The film was a great success all over the world. A contract with the very prestigious Liberty record label followed.

In April 1957 Cochran enjoyed his first Top 20 hit in the UK, 'Sitting in the Balcony'. Two flop singles followed but in September 1958 Cochran released his all-time classic record, 'Summertime Blues'. A telling song about teenage frustration, it entered the Top 20 charts on both sides of the Atlantic.

UK IDOL

From this point on, Eddie Cochran was more successful in the UK than the USA. In 1959 'C'm On Everybody' entered the UK Top 10 – but it didn't even make the Top 30 in the USA. Later that year 'Somethin' Else' became a big UK hit (both of these singles would be covered by the Sex Pistols 20 years later) as did 'Hallelujah I Love Her' in 1960.

Cochran made his UK television debut in 1960 on Jack Good's 'Boy Meets Girl' pop show and did a lengthy tour with fellow rockers Gene Vincent, Billy Fury, Joe Brown and Georgie Fame. The tour was so successful that promoter Larry Parnes extended it by two weeks. Finally, a weary Cochran and Vincent climbed into a cab to take them to the airport and their flight home.

SWAN SONG

The poignantly titled, 'Three Steps to Heaven', was released just after Cochran's death. Eddie Cochran was only 21 when he died – in the country which had adopted him as one of its very favourite rock 'n' roll performers.

JACK GOOD AND LARRY PARNES

TV was important in promoting rock 'n' roll in the UK and Jack Good produced most of the shows that were compulsory viewing for teenagers in the late '50s. 6.5 Special was followed by Oh Boy! and Boy Meets Girl, then Wham!

Amazingly Good predicted the rock video: "It will ultimately become standard practice for every artist to make a film of themselves performing their record. These short films will be sent to TV producers for their programmes." The year was 1959.

Larry Parnes was the man who 'spotted' most of the UK's rock 'n' roll stars. In 1960 he rejected the Beatles as not good enough to back his new find, Billy Fury.

Jack Good was converted to rock 'n' roll when he saw, 'Rock Around The Clock'.

'Singing To My Baby'
August '58.

'The Eddie Cochran Memorial Album'
September '60

'Cherished Memories'
December '62

'The Very Best of Eddie Cochran'
April '70

BO DIDDLEY

In 1951 Elias McDaniel, aged 21, secured his first professional job as a musician in Chicago's 708 Clubs. Astonishingly he had already been playing guitar semi-professionally for over ten years, although only on the street and at parties and dances. Diddley had also enjoyed modest success as a boxer. It was while he was boxing that he was nicknamed 'Bo Diddley'.

MUSIC WINS OUT

Diddley studied classical violin for twelve years and, living in Chicago, had been exposed to the blues style of Muddy Waters who gigged locally. It was hardly surprising that music should take precedence over boxing and Bo began to write songs and develop his musical skills.

In 1955, along with fellow musicians Jerome Green, Frank Kirkland, Lester Davenport and legendary piano player Otis Spann, Diddley took his songs, 'Bo Diddley', 'I'm a Man' and 'You Don't Love Me', to Chicago's Checker record label, owned by Leonard Chess. 'Bo Diddley' was released in June of that year and, with its throbbing jungle rhythm, was an immediate success. An appearance on the prestigious 'Ed Sullivan Show' followed and Diddley was on his way.

Like many other US rock 'n' rollers, he achieved a greater success in the UK than at home.

Diddley is famous for his series of custom-made guitars.

However his singles 'Who Do You Love', 'Crackin' Up', 'Say Man', 'Road Runner' and 'You Can't Judge a Book by Looking at its Cover' all did well, making the US Top 100.

Bo Diddley jams with Ron Wood from the Faces.

DIDDLEY IN THE UK

Diddley was becoming a huge influence on some very important UK bands. The Rolling Stones, Manfred Mann, the Yardbirds, the Animals, the Who and many other groups recorded his songs.

In 1963 Diddley arrived in the UK for a tour with the Everly Brothers and the Rolling Stones. His presence helped to put 'Pretty Thing' and 'Bo Diddley' into the UK charts during that year.

Between 1963 and '69 Diddley spent a great deal of time in the UK, touring and appearing on TV. His albums were now selling better than his singles.

BACK TO BLUES

In 1968 Diddley returned to his blues roots when he recorded the album, 'The Super Blues Band', with Muddy Waters and Little Walter. In the late '60s and early '70s Diddley appeared regularly on the US 'Rock 'n' Roll Revival' shows with fellow stars Chuck Berry, Little Richard and Jerry Lee Lewis. Few hits followed but deserved recognition was on its way.

In 1976 Bo Diddley contributed to RCA Records' 'The 20th Anniversary of Rock 'n' Roll' with Joe Cocker, Alvin Lee, Keith Moon, Billy Joel, Roger McQuinn and many others.

DIDDLEY ON TV

When it started, rock 'n' roll received so much bad press that Diddley's invitation to appear on the 'family' Ed Sullivan Show was good news for the cause. But the rockers didn't always help themselves – and Bo nearly blew it.

TV superstar Ed Sullivan wanted Bo to perform 'Sixteen Tons'. He rehearsed it over and over and the words were written on big cue cards ready for the performance. But as the show went out live, Bo picked up his guitar, ignored the cue cards (and Ed Sullivan's specific request) and played instead his signature tune, 'Bo Diddley'.

Diddley plays a Live Aid charity concert in Philadelphia in 1985.

'Go Bo Diddley'
October '58
'Bo Diddley Is A Gunslinger'
September '61
'Bo Diddley' November '62

'The London Bo Diddley Sessions'
July '73
'The 20th Anniversary of Rock 'n' Roll'
June '91

FATS DOMINO

Antoine Domino was born in 1926 in New Orleans, Louisiana, the home of many excellent rhythm and blues piano players. Fats Domino is probably the very best of them, and almost certainly the most famous. In 1987 he was honoured at the Grammy awards as "one of the most important links between rhythm and blues and rock 'n' roll, a most influential performer whose style of piano playing and 'down home' singing have led the way for generations of performers". His song 'Blueberry Hill' was voted into the Rock 'n' Roll Hall of Fame as one of the best rock 'n' roll songs ever.

FATS HITS THE ROAD

Fats Domino joined Dave Bartholomew's band in 1949 and was soon signed to the Imperial record label. (The nickname 'Fats' was given to Domino by his bass player, Billy Diamond, due to Domino's 16-stone bulk.) Domino's song, 'The Fat Man', sold more than a million copies. Domino hit the road and began his immensely successful career. Hit after hit followed from 1950 to '52.

Domino had married his childhood sweetheart Rose Marie in 1947. Fats had eight brothers and sisters. He and Rose had eight children and Fats' great love of his family eventually restricted his touring schedule.

'Fats Domino – Rock and Rolling!'
August '56
'This Is Fats Domino'
February '57

'Here Stands Fats Domino'
June '57
'My Blue Heaven: The Best of Fats Domino'
February '91

Domino had even more hits in 1953 and '54 which allowed him to indulge in buying the ornate gold and diamond rings he loved. His hands were his living and, adorned, were certainly part of his image. In 1955 Fats won over the new rock 'n' roll audience with a Top 10 hit, 'Ain't That a Shame'.

Domino appeared in four films.

THE UK TAKES NOTICE

It wasn't until 1956 that Domino made a real impact in the UK. But once he had made the breakthrough with 'I'm In Love Again', 'My Blue Heaven' and 'Blueberry Hill' he had a steady stream of hits. In 1957 his songs, 'Honey Chile', 'Blue Monday', 'I'm Walking' and 'Valley of Tears' all entered the UK Top 30. Domino kept writing, kept touring and the hits kept coming.

RICH REWARDS

ALAN FREED

Alan Freed was the rock 'n' roll radio DJ of the '50s and, some believe, the man most responsible for rock 'n' roll's success.

In 1958 Freed arranged a concert at the Boston Arena, featuring Fats Domino, Jerry Lee Lewis, the Crickets and many others. At that time the notion of black and white artists performing together to a mixed audience was contentious, particularly in Boston where racial tension exists even today.

When a white girl climbed on stage and grabbed a black performer all hell broke loose. The police rushed on the stage and the audience was pushed outside where more police were beating up the teenagers. Alan Freed climbed on stage and and yelled, "The police don't want you to have any fun here."

The only person prosecuted was Freed, for inciting a riot.

Two years later Freed was in trouble again – this time on payola charges (accepting bribes to play records).

Freed (right) had a cameo role in the movie, 'Don't Knock The Rock'.

By the '60s Domino had become a very wealthy man and began to take life just a little easier. Tours became less lengthy and the gaps between them and between recording sessions became longer. The hit singles petered out. He still finds the time to appear on TV shows, to make films and play selected venues in the USA (Las Vegas remains a big favourite for him).

Fats Domino can afford to rest upon his laurels. He has produced 36 Top 40 singles and sold just under 100 million records during his 40-year career.

Domino in concert in Paris at the 'Halle That Jazz' festival in 1992.

BILL HALEY

Like so many performers before him, Bill Haley's musical influences were diverse. Born in Michigan in 1925, he came from a musical family. His parents both played and loved country and western music and Haley himself started his career at the age of thirteen with a local country and western band. Two years later he led his own band, playing a mixture of country music and western swing, although Bill was also listening hard to the rhythm and blues pouring out of his local radio station. In 1951 he recorded 'Rocket 88' and 'Rock The Joint'. Bill Haley soon suspected that the heady mix of country music and hard rhythm and blues could be commercially successful and he was right. In 1952 he recorded the pulsating 'Crazy Man Crazy' and two years later 'Shake, Rattle and Roll' earned him a gold record, an award for records which sell in excess of one million.

ROCK AROUND THE CLOCK

But the best was yet to come. 'Rock Around The Clock', recorded by Haley and the Comets in 1955 is possibly the world's best known rock 'n' roll record, eventually selling around 20 million copies. Featured in the film 'Blackboard Jungle', and the inspiration behind Haley's follow-up film of the same name, 'Rock Around The Clock' deserves its status as a rock 'n' roll anthem.

Although 'Rock Around The Clock' represents the zenith of Haley's career, the follow up record, 'See You Later Alligator', was also a huge success and another film, 'Don't Knock The Clock', featuring a whole host of rock 'n' rollers, followed fast. In 1957 Bill Haley visited the UK for the first time, to rapturous acclaim. But his popularity was beginning to wane. Haley was 32 years old and competing with a new generation of younger performers. The 'kiss curl' and tartan jacket image was beginning to look very old-fashioned to his young fans.

Haley plays the Albert Hall, London in May 68.

14

Although Haley continued to tour the world, earning a very comfortable living, no more hit records were to come. Ill-health dogged him and he died from heart problems in February 1981, aged 55. He left a legacy of some of the most enjoyable rock 'n' roll recordings of all time.

When 'Rock Around

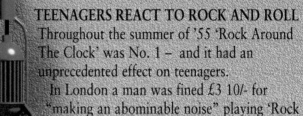

*Haley told the Comets, "Don't just play – **do** something!"*

The Clock' was re-released on its 20th anniversary in 1974 it immediately charted again on both sides of the Atlantic.

"One, two, three o'clock, four o'clock rock, five, six, seven o'clock, eight o'clock rock"...

... everybody can sing the next line!

TEENAGERS REACT TO ROCK AND ROLL

Throughout the summer of '55 'Rock Around The Clock' was No. 1 – and it had an unprecedented effect on teenagers.

In London a man was fined £3 10/- for "making an abominable noise" playing 'Rock Around The Clock' for two and a half hours.

At Princeton University in the USA a student played the record, then another joined in and very soon a riot erupted with students singing and burning rubbish outside the dorms.

When the film 'Blackboard Jungle' was released UK teenagers saw for the first time how to dance to the music. They ended up jiving in the cinema aisles and out into the streets.

In Liverpool police chased 1,000 jiving teenagers a mile across the city centre before turning water hoses on them.

Meanwhile teenagers in the USA wrecked cinemas as soon as 'Rock Around The Clock' was played.

'Rock Around the Clock'
June '56
'Rock and Roll Stage Show'
November '56

'The Very Best of Bill Haley
& His Comets'
July '92

WE'RE GONNA
ROCK AROUND THE CLOCK
Words & Music by MAX C FREEDMAN & JIMMY DE KNIGHT
COLUMBIA PICTURES presents
BILL HALEY
AND HIS COMETS
ROCK AROUND THE CLOCK
THE PLATTERS
(ERNIE FREEMAN COMBO)
TONY MARTINEZ
AND HIS BAND
FREDDIE BELL
AND HIS BELLBOYS
ALAN FREED
JOHNNY JOHNSTON
ALIX TALTON
LISA GAYE · EARL BARTON
HENRY SLATE · JOHN ARCHER
Produced by SAM KATZMAN · Directed by FRED F. SEARS
A CLOVER PRODUCTION
EDWARD KASSNER MUSIC CO. LTD

BUDDY HOLLY

On the morning of 3 February 1959 in Clear Lake, Iowa, USA Buddy Holly climbed aboard a small aeroplane with fellow rock 'n' roll artists The Big Bopper and Ritchie Valens. Their aim was to avoid yet another long, cold trip on the tour bus, so that the three musicians could arrive early enough at the next concert venue to do their washing and catch up with some much needed sleep. The 'Winter Dance Party Tour' had been gruelling. Minutes after take-off the tiny Beechcraft Bonanza plunged to the ground near Mason City, Iowa. All aboard died. Buddy Holly was just 22 years old.

The Big Bopper

Ritchie Valens

The wreckage of the plane that crashed with Holly on board.

THE HITS START COMING

A big admirer of Elvis Presley, Chuck Berry and Little Richard, Holly started playing country and western (C&W) music in 1954. He teamed up with Jerry Allison, Joe Maudlin and Niki Sullivan, and met a man who would have a huge influence on his short career, Norman Petty, producer and songwriter. 'That'll Be The Day' was released in May 1957, and was an instant No. 1 hit on both sides of the Atlantic.

US TEENAGERS IN THE '50s

Bespectacled teenagers the world over breathed a huge sigh of relief when Buddy Holly burst on to the scene as a rock 'n' roll star. At last, here was a popular hero who wore glasses!

It was 1957 and for the first time teenagers were no longer just younger versions of their parents. They had their own language, clothes, social scene and music.

In the USA teenagers met in ice cream parlours, drank ice cream sodas and malted milk and ate pizza pie. They drove in to movies and to the first McDonalds. Boys customized their cars whilst girls borrowed their parents' cars to cruise and hang out in the drive-ins.

Boys had sideburns with their quiffed hair tapering into a point at the back of the neck, called a DA (duck's ass). Their shoes were suede (more often white than blue!).

Girls wore trousers, jeans that stopped short of the ankle, called pedal pushers (always with a side zip – flies were for boys!), white ankle socks and pony tail hairdos.

'Cat', 'hip', 'chick', 'cool' were all part of the new teen-speak and came from language previously used mainly by blacks in the '20s.

Cruising past a drive-in movie in the US in the '50s.

Holly himself was an accomplished writer and hit after hit followed during 1957 and '58. Buddy Holly and the Crickets made a rare and welcome visit to the UK in 1958.

TIRED OF TOURING

Holly's touring schedule was exhausting in the '50s. He fell out with Norman Petty, who demanded a credit and royalties on all Holly's songs. This and Holly's move to New York, were both factors in his split from the Crickets. Now two versions of the band were on tour, Buddy Holly and his new backing group, and the Crickets. Holly was weary of travelling by 1959 but, short of money, he hauled himself on to the road to pay the bills.

He had recorded 'It Doesn't Matter Anymore', written by Paul Anka. The song was an ironic and sad posthumous success for Holly, topping the charts in the USA and the UK.

STILL REMEMBERED

Don McLean in his 1971 hit record, 'American Pie', described Holly's death as "the day the music died".

The musical, 'Buddy', about Holly's life is a big success in London and Europe. His music sounds as fresh today as in 1959.

'Buddy Holly'
July '58

'20 Golden Greats'
March '78
'20 Love Songs'
August '82

The Crickets in 1958 were (from left to right) Jerry Allison (18), Joe Maudlin (18) and Holly (21).

JERRY LEE LEWIS

Described as the 'wildest rock 'n' roller bar none', Jerry Lee Lewis's nickname was 'The Killer', earned because of his exuberant stage presence. Lewis was born in Louisiana in 1935. He taught himself to play the piano in just two weeks at the age of 13. Three years later he married the first of his six wives. His personal life has been tumultuous: two of his wives died in mysterious circumstances, two of his children died in tragic accidents and two of his marriages were bigamous.

THE BREAKTHROUGH

In 1956, when Jerry was 21 years old, he and his father went to the legendary Sun Studios in Memphis, where Elvis Presley and Carl Perkins had started their recording careers. Lewis persuaded owner Sam Phillips to record his powerful, 'Whole Lotta Shakin' Goin' On'. Banned by many radio stations, it sold a modest amount until Lewis got the break he really needed. He was invited to appear on the nationally broadcast 'Steve Allen Show'. Sales of the single immediately escalated. Six million copies later, Lewis found himself at the top of both the rhythm and blues (R&B) and country and western (C&W) charts.

MILLION DOLLAR QUARTET

Christmas 1956 saw Jerry Lee Lewis at the Sun Studios in Memphis, where the so-called Million Dollar Quartet were recorded playing together for the first and only time.

Elvis was home for Christmas. (He'd given his and hers cadillacs to his parents.) He went along to Sun Studios where he met up with Lewis, Johnny Cash and Carl Perkins – and the Million Dollar Quartet had their only jamming session.

When the tape of the session was released 25 years later, most people agreed that the music was awful!

Lewis is known for his 'pumpin' piano' style.

'Jerry Lee Lewis'
January '59
'Jerry Lee Lewis Vol Two'
May '62
'The Greatest Live Show On Earth (Live)'
May '65

'The Return of Rock'
July '65
'Killer Hits – The Original Classics'
May '95

To cap a highly successful year, he then appeared in a film with Carl Perkins, Fats Domino and many other R&B stars, entitled 'Jamboree'. He toured incessantly but still found the time to marry bigamously his 13-year-old second cousin, Myra Gale Brown, the daughter of his bass player.

THE SCANDAL

1958 brought more success, but also big problems. When Lewis arrived in the UK with his child bride for a major tour, the British media expressed its horror at what it saw as a scandal. The tour was cancelled. Lewis's career began to stall.

Lewis toured the UK again in 1962 and '64, and in 1966 played Iago in Jack Good's musical, 'Othello', in London's West End. By now alcohol and drugs were badly affecting Lewis and his personal life was in turmoil.

Lewis and his young wife, Myra, face the cameras in London.

In 1968 Lewis turned to C&W and for the next 20 years had a successful career. Although he never quite left rock 'n' roll behind him, it never dominated his music again. More divorces and marriages followed and in 1976 Lewis crashed his Rolls Royce, shot his bass player and was arrested outside Elvis Presley's home, demanding to see Elvis whilst armed with a gun.

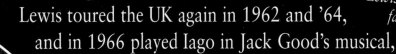

Lewis performs at a C&W festival in Wembley, London in 1982.

STILL GOING STRONG

A larger than life character, 'The Killer' still tours the world at the age of 63, causing mayhem, but richly entertaining thousands of fans.

ROY ORBISON

Roy Orbison's image and stage presence were very subdued for a rock 'n' roll star. Orbison, dressed in black, his eyes concealed by his trademark sunglasses, stayed glued to the centre stage. His rather high pitched, quavering voice was unique and seemed almost more suited to light opera than to rock music.

SONGWRITER TURNED SINGER

In 1960, after rather a slow start to his show business career, Orbison wrote and released his first massive hit. A song he had actually written for either Elvis or the Everly Brothers to record, the dramatic 'Only the Lonely' was a huge hit for Orbison on both sides of the Atlantic. Its success was quickly repeated. Many more singles made the charts in the USA and the UK in the '60s, selling millions of copies.

In 1962 Orbison released 'Dream Baby' and, like so many rock 'n' rollers, found that the young people in the UK had taken him to their hearts.

*Orbison appeared **without** his glasses in a movie, 'The Fastest Guitar Alive', in 1966.*

In September 1963 he toured England. 'In Dreams' was a big hit in the same year and it seemed that Roy Orbison was destined to stay in the fast lane.

Orbison collects his award from the Hall of Fame in 1987.

TRAGEDY AND TOURS

The hits followed with 'Blue Bayou', 'It's Over' and possibly his best known release, 'Oh Pretty Woman', which sold over seven million copies and made him very wealthy.

But personal tragedy was to strike, not once but twice. In 1966 his wife was killed in an accident whilst the two of them were riding their motorbikes. Orbison threw himself into a tough touring schedule. He was beginning to recover from this dreadful loss when two of his three children died in a fire at his Nashville home. Devastated, Roy coped in the same way as he had before – work and more work! He toured the world for the next decade, rarely giving himself a break from his punishing regime.

A TRIBUTE

Orbison's hits dried up but other artists recorded his excellent songs. In 1987 he was inducted into the Rock 'n' Roll Hall of Fame in New York. A richly-deserved TV tribute followed, honouring his 26-year career at the forefront of rock 'n' roll.

In 1988 Orbison joined Bob Dylan, Jeff Lynne, George Harrison and Tom Petty in the Traveling Wilburys. Their album entered the Top 20 in both the UK and the USA. Orbison died from a heart attack soon afterwards.

'Lonely and Blue' October '61
'Crying' May '62
'Roy Orbison's Greatest Hits' October '62
'In Dreams' November '63
'The Singles Collection 1965-1973' May '89
'Golden Decade Boxed Set' July '90
'The Golden Years 1960-1969' June '93

TWELVE BAR BLUES

In blues, a 12 bar structure, 3 phrases of 4 bars, soon became the norm. A blues in 'E', a key popular with guitarists, would be as below:

There are many variations on this sequence and, of course, not all blues pieces use this structure.

Bar:	1	2	3	4
Chord:	E	E	E	E
	5	6	7	8
	A	A	E	E
	9	10	11	12
	B	A	E	E

If you have a keyboard with automatic rhythms find a blues or R&B setting and switch on the 'single fingered chord' facility. Start the rhythm and play 'E' at the bottom end of the keyboard, counting out 4 bars of 'E' as follows:

E234 E234 E234 E234

Now try the whole 12 bars as written out right:

E234	E234	E234	E234
A234	A234	E234	E234
B234	A234	E234	fill-in*

* Press the fill-in button here.

ELVIS PRESLEY

The only survivor of twins, Elvis Aaron Presley was born in Tupelo, Mississippi on 8 January 1935 and died just over 42 years later in Memphis on 16 August 1977. Elvis Presley drifted through school and had several menial jobs. His family was poor and Elvis was keen to contribute to their finances. He could hardly have dreamt how great that contribution would become.

ELVIS IS SPOTTED

In 1953 Elvis Presley dropped into the Sun Sudios in Memphis to make a record as a present for his mother.

Elvis and Priscilla appeared in the movie, 'This is Elvis'.

ELVIS SOUNDS BLACK

Rock 'n' roll's roots were in black gospel music. Sam Phillips felt he had only to find a white boy who could sing black music and he would have it made. Elvis was that boy. When he was interviewed on local radio Elvis was asked which school he had attended – so that the listeners would hear it was a school for whites.

When Elvis appeared on the Ed Sullivan TV show in 1956, his gyrating act in front of screaming teenagers caused an outcry. Sullivan later insisted that Elvis be filmed only from the waist up. But the audience still screamed as hard as ever.

Owner Sam Phillips spotted his huge talent. He introduced Elvis to three musicians, Scotty Moore, Bill Black and D J Fontana, and Elvis released five singles on the Sun label. None sold well but Elvis's talent was recognised by RCA Records, a large record company in New York. They paid Sam Phillips $35,000 (worth about £15,000,000 in today's money!) for Presley's contract and the right to release all future records by Elvis.

CALLED UP

Elvis's career dramatically took off in 1956 when 'Heartbreak Hotel' topped the US charts for eight weeks. Nine No. 1 hits followed for Presley but in 1958 his career was rudely interrupted when he was called up by the US Army. Before joining, Elvis recorded several songs which were hits while he was away.

Elvis may be the most famous US soldier.

MOVIES

On March 1961 Elvis returned to civilian life and started a new career as a movie star. Some fans think his talent was wasted over the next decade as he appeared in a stream of mediocre films.

Elvis starred in the movie, 'Paradise Hawaiian Style'.

MORE HITS

In 1968, following his marriage to Priscilla and the birth of their daughter, Lisa-Marie, he made a comeback on an NBC TV Special. Between 1970 and '73 eleven hit singles followed and in 1973 Elvis performed in a live worldwide TV programme from Hawaii. All the proceeds went to charity and the soundtrack album sold over a million copies.

DIVORCE, DRUGS, DEATH

Things were going wrong for Elvis in his personal life. He was divorced from Priscilla in 1972. Five years later, due to drug problems and an appallingly unhealthy diet, he died at his home, Graceland.

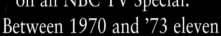

'Elvis Presley'
March '56
'Rock 'n' Roll No. 1'
October '56
'Rock 'n' Roll No. 2' April '57
'Loving You' August '57

'Elvis's Golden Records Volumes One to Five'
September '81
'The Definitive Rock 'n' Roll Album'
November '93

CLIFF RICHARD

"It was the most crude exhibitionism ever seen on British TV. Revolting. Hardly the kind of performance any parent would wish his children to witness!" This was how a journalist described the debut television performance of Harry Webb on 13 September 1958. 40 years later, Webb was knighted.

BRITAIN'S ELVIS

Richard started his singing career as Britain's answer to Elvis Presley, and he certainly deserves his place in the annals of rock 'n' roll history, although he didn't remain a rock 'n' roller for very long.

Harry Webb was born in India in 1940 and came to England with his parents when he was eight years old. An uneventful childhood followed but in 1957 Webb discovered the thrilling sounds of US rock 'n' roll! In one of several parallels with the career of his idol, Elvis Presley, Webb recorded a private demonstration disc with his new band, the Drifters. Gigs at London's renowned 2Is Club followed and Harry Webb became Cliff Richard.

In July 1958, Cliff and the Drifters won a prestigious talent competition at the Gaumont Cinema in London's Shepherd's Bush, and Richard's agent, George Ganjon, persuaded the major UK record label EMI to listen to him.

Cliff started out playing guitar but soon concentrated on vocals.

'Cliff'
November '52
'Cliff Sings'
November '59
'Me and My Shadows' October '60

'Rock On With Cliff Richard'
June '87
'Cliff Richard:
The Rock 'n' Roll Years'
October '97

EMI's man Norrie Paramor liked what he heard and Richard recorded his first single. The song chosen for Cliff to record was called 'Schoolboy Crush' – the throwaway B side of the record, 'Move It', was written by Drifter Ian Samwell during his bus journey to the recording studio. When the record was released everybody preferred this song. 'Move It' is still considered to be one of the most authentic UK rock 'n' roll records ever made.

THE SHADOWS

In October 1958 Cliff made his infamous debut on the popular 'Oh Boy' TV show. Producer Jack Good moulded Richard's image and his popularity rocketed. Cliff recruited a new line-up for his backing band, consisting of guitarists Hank Marvin and Bruce Welch, bass player Jet Harris, and drummer Tony Meehan who quickly changed their name from the Drifters to the Shadows. They achieved huge success as an instrumental group, at one stage knocking Cliff off the No 1 spot with 'Apache'.

The Shadows and Cliff, who's holding his gold disc for 'Congratulations', in 1968.

TEDDY BOYS AND GIRLS

When not tuning in to Radio Luxembourg on their transistor radios teenagers in the UK met in coffee bars and listened to their music on the new juke boxes. The most famous coffee bar of all was the 2I's in London's Soho. Many rock 'n' roll stars had their first break there, including Cliff Richard.

Because space was so limited in these bars, the hand jive was born – a dance that was performed seated or standing but only the hands move!

The Teddy Boy look at the time was slicked-back hair with a DA, long jackets, drainpipe trousers and heavy, crepe-soled shoes. Teddy Girls wore stiletto heels, pencil skirts, polo-necks and had back-combed 'beehive' hair. By the mid-'50s girls wore big skirts with stiff petticoats – perfect for jiving – or tight, ankle length trousers.

All a far cry from the post-war fashions of their parents.

A curious teenager checks out the Teddy Boy look.

CAREER MOVE

Cliff had a string of hit records but by 1960, fearing that Cliff's 'Elvis' phase would date, Paramor persuaded him to record the more middle-of-the-road, 'Living Doll'. Cliff didn't like it but when the song gave him his first No. 1 hit he realised that a new career, aimed at a much wider age range, would be a smart move.

After a career lasting four decades and countless hit singles, he was right, but many of his original fans felt that Cliff's post-rock 'n' roll work lacked the appeal of his early singles. Respectable Sir Cliff may have become, but perhaps his two year reign as one of Britain's finest rock 'n' rollers was a little too short!

LITTLE RICHARD

Richard Wayne Penniman hardly warranted his nickname 'little'. One of the most flamboyant and egoistic performers on the rock 'n' roll scene, Little Richard enjoyed a spectacular career during the '50s and '60s. Born in 1935 in Macon, Georgia, Little Richard came from a familiar background for a rock 'n' roller. Blues and gospel music greatly influenced him and his large family (he had eleven brothers and sisters) were all heavily involved in the church, singing and playing spiritual music.

TEENAGE BEGINNINGS

Richard's unique talent as a singer and piano player soon emerged. His first efforts in the RCA Victor recording studios at the tender age of 16 were not successful, but, considering his age, the eight songs he recorded showed a surprising maturity and promise.

In 1954 Little Richard met rock 'n' roll star Lloyd Price who suggested that he send tapes of his songs to Los Angeles record company, Specialty Records. In the following year Richard recorded the song for Specialty which would launch his international career, 'Tutti Frutti', with one of the most bizarre first lines ever written, 'Awop bop a loo bop a lop bam boom, tutti frutti'. He sold all publishing and royalty rights to the song for $50. It entered the US charts, peaked at No. 17, and eventually sold over three million copies!

'Here's Little Richard'
July '57
'Little Richard 2' December '58
'The Fabulous Little Richard'
May '59

'Little Richard is Back'
February '65
'20 Classic Cuts' December '86
'The Collection'
July '89

Little Richard went back into the studio in 1956 with his band of Earl Palmer (drums), Lee Allen (sax), Frank Field (bass) and other renowned New Orleans musicians.

Between 1956 and '58 Richard could do no wrong, recording a stream of hugely successful international hits.

Richard's appearance in the film,
'The Girl Can't Help It' promoted his outrageous reputation.

TOM EWELL · JAYNE MANSFIELD · EDMOND O'BRIEN in THE GIRL CAN'T HELP IT
with Guest stars JULIE LONDON · RAY ANTHONY · BARRY GORDON and featuring HENRY JONES
Produced and Directed by FRANK TASHLIN   Screenplay by FRANK TASHLIN and HERBERT BAKER
A 20th CENTURY-FOX CINEMASCOPE PICTURE IN EASTMAN COLOUR   Cert 'U'

RICHARD AND RELIGION

The world seemed at Little Richard's feet, but a terrifying incident during a European flight pitched him into a completely different direction. An engine fire convinced him that he was going to die and he pledged that, if saved, he would devote his life to God. He kept his promise. Little Richard went to college, earned a BA degree and was ordained as a minister of the Seventh Day Adventist Church. He stayed in the church until 1963.

FAME AGAIN

Richard returned to music and spent years touring Europe with the then little-known bands, the Rolling Stones and the Beatles who were very familiar with his material. As both bands became hugely successful in the USA in the late '60s, their loud praise of Little Richard had a great spin off for him. Work flooded in and he hit the road.

US graduates demonstrate rock 'n' roll's popularity.

Little Richard was successful again – although he never achieved the heady heights he had enjoyed in the '50s and '60s.

Despite a brief return to the church after the death of his brother in the mid-'70s, the '90s sees Little Richard still playing, still recording and still, at the age of 63, pounding those keyboards all over the world.

GENE VINCENT

Eugene Vincent Craddock was born in Norfolk, Virginia in 1935. He joined the navy when he was in his teens, lying about his age in order to enlist. When he was 20 years old, his leg was seriously injured in a motorbike accident. Gene was bored and unable to work and so, as he had an excellent voice, his mother advised him to become a singer. The huge US label Capitol was on the lookout for an artist to compete with Elvis Presley. They held a talent contest and Vincent won. He promptly recorded two songs, 'Women Love' and a song he bought for $25 from his friend, Don Graves, called 'Be Bop A Lula'.

FINE START

In 1956 'Women Love' was released as the A side of the record and earned Gene Vincent a $10,000 fine for 'public lewdness and obscenity'. Nobody cared though, because 'Be Bop A Lula' was the song all the DJs chose to play. The record shot to No. 7 on the US charts and went on to sell a million copies.

Between 1956 and '58 Gene Vincent had many more hits and worked with an excellent backing group called the Blue Caps, who were revered in their own right by rock 'n' roll fans. Their first lead guitar player, Cliff Gallup, was extremely talented, and as recently as 1993, acclaimed British rock guitarist Jeff Beck recorded a tribute to him with the UK band, Big Town Playboys. Eventually Vincent was more popular and successful in Europe than in the USA.

'Gene Vincent & His Blue Caps' April '57
'Gene Vincent Rocks and The Blue Caps Roll' December '57
'A Gene Vincent Record Date' April '58
'Sounds Like Gene Vincent' October '58
'Crazy Times' May '60
'The Gene Vincent Box Set' September '90

Vincent returns to the USA after the car crash.

'Lotta Lovin', 'Race With The Devil', 'Blue Jean Bop' and 'Dance To The Bop' all did well for him during the late '50s.

COCHRAN'S CRASH
Sadly, during a tour of the UK in 1960, Vincent was badly injured in a serious car accident which killed fellow rocker, the hugely talented Eddie Cochran. Recovering from his injuries took months.

Vincent and the Blue Caps rock in the film, 'The Girl Can't Help It.'

Vincent then chose to make his home in the UK, and earned a reasonable living touring there and in Europe. He returned to the USA many times, taking part in the regular 'Rock 'n' Roll Revival' shows which were very popular in the 1970s, with fellow heroes Little Richard, Bo Diddley, Jerry Lee Lewis and many other famous rock 'n' roll performers.

BACK HOME
Vincent's serious injuries, his years of alcohol and drug abuse and the strain of constant touring finally took their toll. In 1971, back in the USA, Vincent was taken to hospital with internal bleeding caused by a perforated stomach ulcer. Gene Vincent died on 12 October 1971 in Newhall, California. He was just 36 years old.

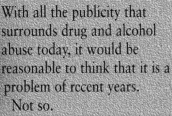

DRINK AND DRUGS
With all the publicity that surrounds drug and alcohol abuse today, it would be reasonable to think that it is a problem of recent years.

Not so.

Back in the 1950s some of the greatest of the rock 'n' rollers paid the highest penalty for their drug-taking and drinking habits – an early death. So much talent and brilliant music is lost to us as a result. Over the years the drugs may change but, sadly, the end is too often the same. There is a lesson to be learnt from the short lives of these revellers of the past.

Vincent visits a London club just a few months before his death, looking older than his 36 years.

GAZETTEER

Billy Fury

There were many, many rock 'n' roll heroes to be found on both sides of the Atlantic and no one book could feature them all!

UK ROCK 'N' ROLLERS

In the UK Cliff Richard was not our only credible rock 'n' roller. Ronald Wycherly, a Liverpool tugboat man, talked his way backstage during a Marty Wilde concert to request an audition with promoter, Larry Parnes, and found himself performing for the rest of the tour, renamed Billy Fury. He recorded 'Sound of Fury' which is generally thought to be the finest rock 'n' roll album ever recorded in this country, plus many hit singles, including the classic, 'Half Way to Paradise'. Tommy Steele enjoyed a short but spectacular rock 'n' roll career. He soon became a popular all-round entertainer.

Duane Eddy

INSTRUMENTAL GROUPS

During the 1960s there were literally dozens of popular instrumental groups working in the USA and the UK. The Ventures ('Walk Don't Run'), the Champs ('Tequila'), Duane Eddy ('Peter Gunn', 'Rebel Rouser' and many other hits) and Johnny and the Hurricanes ('Red River Rock') were very successful in the USA. In the UK one group, the Shadows, dominated the rock 'n' roll scene. Cliff Richard's backing group in the mid-'60s, they enjoyed dozens of Top 20 hits in their own right.

Carl Perkins

BLUE SUEDE SHOES

Arguably the greatest performers were found on the other side of the Atlantic. The list is almost endless. Carl Perkins wrote and recorded one of the greatest rockabilly songs of all time, 'Blue Suede Shoes'.

Ruth Brown

Elvis Presley recorded it later. Carl was one of the most gifted rock 'n' roll performers, although his career stalled after an awful car crash in the '60s. He died in 1998.

The Ronettes

ROCK 'N' ROLL WOMEN

Many very talented women performers were extremely successful. Some were solo singers, others were members of duos or trios. LaVern Baker and Ruth Brown came from spiritual music backgrounds whereas the Shirelles, the Crystals, the Ronettes, Little Eva, Brenda Lee and Connie Francis were pop stars who strongly demonstrated their rock 'n' roll roots.

Connie Francis

BROTHERS

Other important rock 'n' roll stars included the Everly Brothers, a sublimely talented singing duo who unfortunately couldn't stand each other and for decades stayed in separate hotels during tours. Two other sets of brothers were very popular: the Isley Brothers and the Righteous Brothers, most famous for their beautiful recording of 'You've Lost That Loving Feeling'.

Everly brothers

The Righteous Brothers

HARMONY GROUPS

Frankie Lymon, Danny and the Juniors and the witty Coasters all proved that there was a place in the charts for harmony groups singing about teenage problems.

Rock 'n' roll was dismissed by the parents of at least two generations of teenagers as a fad that would last for months at the most. Nearly 50 years on, its appeal is as enduring as ever.

Tommy Steele

INDEX

PHOTOGRAPHIC CREDITS Abbreviations: t-top, m-middle, b-bottom, r-right, l-left, c-centre.

Front cover c, 3, 22t & b & 22-23 – Kobal Collection. Front cover bl & br, 10-11, 11t & 13b – Frank Spooner Pictures. Front cover bm, 5, 9, 12, 14 both, 14-15, 17b, 18t, 19 both, 22m, 24 both. 24-25, 25b, 29b & 31b – Hulton Getty Collection. 4-5, 6t, 6-7, 8 both, 10 both, 16-17, 18b, 20 both, 20-21, 21, 28t, 30 all, 30-31 & 31 all – Retna Pictures. 7 – Delilah / Universal (courtesy Kobal). 8-9, 13t & m, 15b, 26 both, 27ml & 28-29 – Ronald Grant Archive. 11b, 15t, 16 all, 17m, 18-19, 25m, 27mr & 29tl – Corbis / Bettman. 12-13 – 20th Century Fox (courtesy Kobal). 23 – Paramount (courtesy Kobal)